OFFICIAL SQA PAST PAPERS WITH ANSWERS

INTERMEDIATE 2

INFORMATION SYSTEMS 2006-2009

SQA

BrightRED PUBLISHING

First exam published in 2006.
Published by Bright Red Publishing Ltd, 6 Stafford Street, Edinburgh EH3 7AU
tel: 0131 220 5804 fax: 0131 220 6710 info@brightredpublishing.co.uk www.brightredpublishing.co.uk

ISBN 978-1-84948-045-1

A CIP Catalogue record for this book is available from the British Library.

Bright Red Publishing is grateful to the copyright holders, as credited on the final page of the book, for permission to use their material. Every effort has been made to trace the copyright holders and to obtain their permission for the use of copyright material. Bright Red Publishing will be happy to receive information allowing us to rectify any error or omission in future editions.

INTERMEDIATE 2

2006

[BLANK PAGE]

X216/201

NATIONAL QUALIFICATIONS 2006

THURSDAY, 1 JUNE
9.00 AM – 10.30 AM

INFORMATION SYSTEMS
INTERMEDIATE 2

Attempt Sections 1 and 2 and **one part** of Section 3.

Sections 1 and 2 — Attempt all questions within these sections.

Section 3 — This section has three parts:

Part A—Applied Multimedia

Part B—Expert Systems

Part C—The Internet

Choose **one** part of this section and attempt all of the questions within that part.

Read all questions carefully.

Write your answers in the answer book provided. Do not write on the question paper.

Write as neatly as possible.

SCOTTISH QUALIFICATIONS AUTHORITY

SECTION 1

Marks

Attempt all questions in this section.

1. Maria wants to change the format of some text using a word processing package.

Suggest **two** changes she could make to the text. **2**

2. Two data validation processes are a *presence check* and *restricted choice*.

Describe what these **two** processes are. **2**

3. State **one** method which may be used by organisations to ensure that data which has been entered is not lost. **1**

4. Which type of application software would you recommend for the production of annual sales information? **1**

5. The Data Protection Act (1998) gives certain rights to data subjects.

State **two** of these rights. **2**

6. A video rental shop stores details about films for rent in a database.

Here is an example of one record.

Film ID:	F19654		
Film Title:	Star Wars		
Date of Release:	21/03/1977		
Director:	George Lucas		
Genre:	☐ Action	☐ Comedy	☐ Romance
	☒ Sci-Fi	☐ Children	

Suggest the most suitable data type for the fields:

(*a*) Film ID **1**

(*b*) Date of release. **1**

7. What name is given to the process of analysing data to remove multi-value fields? **1**

Marks

8. Here is an extract from a database showing the players in one football club.

Name of Football Club	:	Aberdeen
Name of Stadium	:	Pittodrie
Year Founded	:	1903
Current Players	:	H. Priest
		F. Banderton
		M. McGinty
		K. Gold

State the relationship that exists between the club and the players. **1**

9. The spreadsheet below shows data about crisp packets sold from a class tuck shop.

	A	B	C	D
1	Flavour	Quantity	Cost	Total Cost
2	Cheese & Onion	4	0·38	1·52
3	Prawn Cocktail	5	0·35	1·75
4	Smokey Bacon	3	0·35	1·05
5	Salt N Vinegar	6	0·35	2·1

After formatting the spreadsheet looks like this.

	A	B	C	D
1	**Flavour**	**Quantity**	**Cost**	**Total Cost**
2	Cheese & Onion	4	0·38	£1·52
3	Prawn Cocktail	5	0·35	£1·75
4	Smokey Bacon	3	0·35	£1·05
5	Salt N Vinegar	6	0·35	£2·10

State **two** formatting functions that have been carried out on the spreadsheet. **2**

10. What is meant by a Boolean field type? **1**

Total for Section 1 (15)

[*END OF SECTION 1*]

Marks

SECTION 2

Attempt all questions in this section.

11. Vanhire is a caravan club that rents caravans in different areas.

Vanhire keeps a record of caravans and their sites on a paper-based system. A sample of the data is shown below.

Site and Caravan

Site ID	Site Name	Location	Caravan ID	No of Beds	Energy type	Cost per week
850	Oronsay	Argyle	12 854	4 12	Gas Electric	£100 £275
755	Evanson	Lothians	234 198	6 4	Gas Gas	£132 £198

(*a*) The club wants to move from a paper-based system to a computer based system. State the one to many relationship that exists in this table. **1**

(*b*) Give **two** problems that could arise when multi-valued fields are used in a database. **2**

(*c*) Identify and remove the multi-value fields from the above table and represent the contents as two entities with suitable names. **4**

(*d*) Identify all primary and foreign keys. **3**

(10)

12. Aisha keeps a record of her music CDs in a manual database. She wants to create an electronic database for her CDs so that it will take up less room.

(*a*) Give **two** other advantages of the electronic database over the manual system. **2**

(*b*) Aisha wants to sort her CDs by their title, but does not know how to do a sort, so she consults the *on-line help*.

What is meant by "on-line help"? **1**

(*c*) The sort function gives her the choice of listing songs in ascending or descending order.

Which should she choose if she wants the songs in alphabetical order? **1**

(*d*) Aisha is using a flat file database.

(i) What is a flat file database? **1**

(ii) State **one** disadvantage of using a flat file database. **1**

(6)

Marks

13. ITBrain is an agency involved in training journalists to use different types of application software for creating a magazine.

(*a*) Health and Safety regulations are taken into consideration when designing training rooms for ITBrain.

(i) State **two** examples of Health and Safety regulations that have to be considered when these rooms are being designed. **2**

(ii) State **one** example of a type of application software that might be taught by ITBrain and describe how it can be used in creating the magazine. **1**

(*b*) The details of the journalists that are involved in these courses are stored electronically.

(i) What type of software application would be most suitable for this purpose? **1**

(ii) Give a reason for your answer. **1**

(*c*) State **two** ways in which ITBrain can fulfil its legal responsibilities when storing the journalists' personal details electronically. **2**

(7)

14. A car dealership has showrooms in four Scottish cities: Glasgow, Edinburgh, Dundee and Aberdeen.

(*a*) A *centralised database* for the company is located in their head office in Stirling.

(i) What is meant by a "centralised database"? **1**

(ii) State **two** advantages of a centralised database for this organisation. **2**

(iii) State **one** disadvantage for the car dealership. **1**

(*b*) The Information and Communications Technology (ICT) manager based in Stirling will have to prepare standard strategies for ICT within the organisation.

(i) Suggest what **two** of the strategies might be. **2**

(ii) Choose **one** of the strategies and say how it might impact on the organisation. **1**

(7)

Total for Section 2 (30)

[*END OF SECTION 2*]

[Turn over

SECTION 3

Marks

PART A—Applied Multimedia

15. A software company wants to produce a multimedia application for use by primary school pupils.

(*a*) (i) State **two** aspects the company should consider during the analysis stage of development. **2**

(ii) Explain why each aspect is considered. **2**

(*b*) Suggest a suitable medium for delivery of the multimedia application and give a reason for your choice. **2**

(6)

16. The software company's multimedia application includes a screen that will help the pupils to select the section for their age group.

(*a*) What type of user interface should the designer create? **1**

(*b*) The project manager decides that there should be background music included in the application.

Which type of media specialist should he employ to provide this? **1**

(*c*) Music files use a lot of backing storage space.

Describe **two** methods by which the storage requirements for these files could be reduced. **2**

(4)

17. Sara is a member of the software company's project team and is responsible for the screen design of the multimedia application.

(*a*) What would Sara's job title be? **1**

(*b*) Sara has produced two similar layouts (please refer to Figures 1 and 2 on *Page seven*). One has been designed for children aged three to six years of age. The other is for children aged seven and eight.

(i) Which of the two layouts (Figure 1 or Figure 2) is more suitable for the younger aged child? **1**

(ii) Explain why this layout is more suitable for the younger children with reference to

(A) the layout of the screen elements; **1**

(B) the navigation between the screens. **1**

(*c*) Suggest **two** ways in which the user interface of the application may be improved. **2**

(*d*) Using the diagrams on *Page seven*, explain how the following design principles have been applied to the multimedia application.

(i) The quantity of text used. **1**

(ii) The use of white space. **1**

(8)

Question 17 (continued)

Figure 1

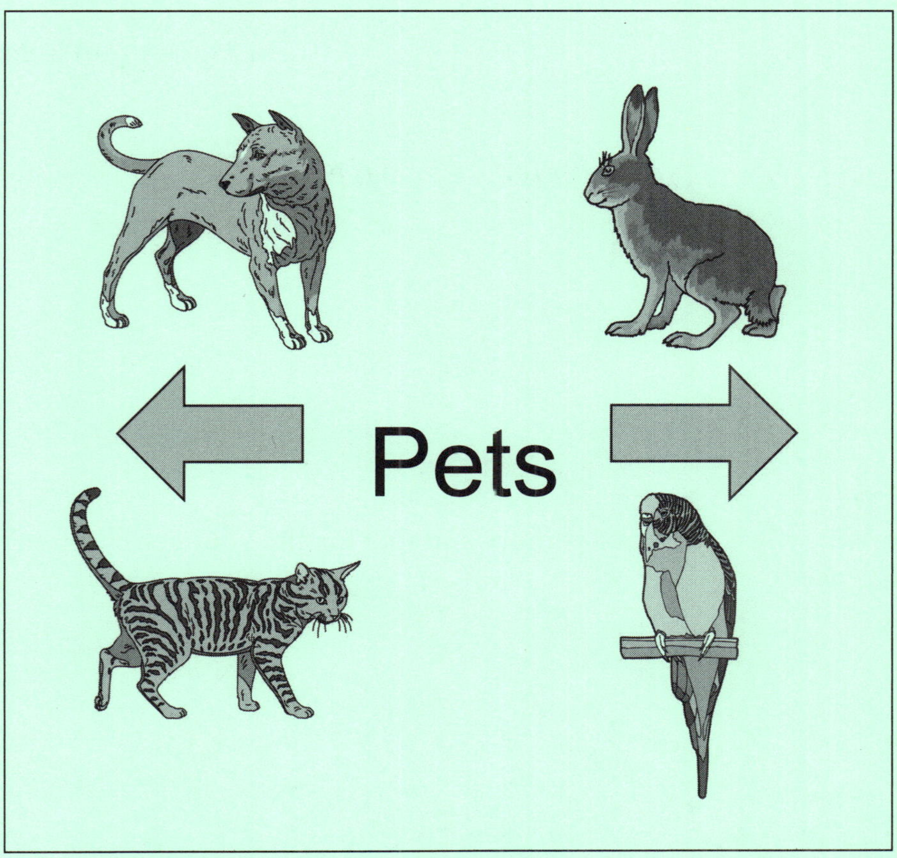

Figure 2

[Turn over

Marks

18. David, a recently appointed multimedia programmer, has joined the project team.

(*a*) What is the role of the multimedia programmer? **1**

(*b*) David decides to use an *authoring package* to create the multimedia application because it will include lots of loop and branches.

(i) State **two** types of "authoring package" David could use. **1**

(ii) Give **one** reason why David would not use a *presentation package*. **1**

(*c*) The subject expert has included a number of graphics taken from a variety of websites.

(i) Why would David be concerned about including these in the multimedia application? **1**

(ii) What piece of legislation governs the use of materials taken from other websites? **1**

(*d*) Once the multimedia application has been completed, the user documentation is written.

(i) Name **one** piece of documentation included here. **1**

(ii) Give **one** reason for the inclusion of this piece. **1**

(7)

Total for Section 3 Part A (25)

[*END OF SECTION 3—PART A*]

SECTION 3

Marks

PART B—Expert Systems

19. Jobchoice is software used by school students to find out about career options. The program poses questions to the students about their interests and qualifications. The students enter their reponses by clicking options on the screen.

(*a*) (i) State which component of the expert system is responsible for displaying the questions and obtaining the answers from the students. **1**

(ii) Describe **one** other function of this component. **1**

(iii) Name **one** other component of an expert system and describe its function. **2**

(*b*) There are four categories of expert systems.

Identification of medical problems is an example of an expert system that gives *diagnosis*.

(i) Which category of expert system best describes Jobchoice? **1**

(ii) State the most appropriate category of expert system for the following expert systems

(A) Identifying different types of colleges;

(B) Organising a rota for interviewing students. **2**

(7)

20. Here is part of a factor table showing knowledge to be entered into an expert system.

Number of Sides	Are all the angles right angles?	Are all the sides equal in length?	Name of Shape
4	Yes	Yes	Square
4	Yes	No	Rectangle
4	No	Yes	Rhombus
4	No	No	Parallelogram
5	No	Yes	Pentagon

The expert system is created using an *expert system shell*.

(*a*) What is an "expert system shell"? **1**

(*b*) Write a rule to represent a rhombus from the knowledge in the table. **3**

[Turn over

Marks

20. (continued)

The diagram below represents a consultation from the expert system once it has been created.

How many sides are there?

?? 4

Are all the angles right angles?

?? yes

Are all the sides equal in length?

?? no

(*c*) State the conclusion reached by the system following this consultation. **1**

(*d*) When a question is asked a button labelled 'Explain' is displayed like this:

How many sides are there?

??

Explain

Give **one** reason for including this button on the screen. **1**

(*e*) An alternative to creating an expert system would be to enter the information in the factor table into a database.

How many fields would the database have? **1**

(*f*) Both an expert system and a database deal with *data* and *information*.

An expert system also deals with *knowledge*.

From the factor table identify

(i) an item of **data**;

(ii) a piece of **information**;

(iii) a piece of **knowledge**. **3**

(10)

Marks

21. An on-line travel agency decides to create an expert system to allow holiday makers to select suitable hotels for their vacation.

The first stage of developing the expert system is called *knowledge acquisition.*

(*a*) Outline what is involved at this stage of the development process and which personnel are involved. **2**

(*b*) The travel agency wants to include a photograph of each hotel in the expert system. Is this legal? Give a reason for your answer. **1**

(*c*) Here is an example of a rule used in the system:

Suggested Hotel IS Palm Beach Court IF
Distance from beach IS less than 2 km AND
Leisure facilities ARE required.

(i) Which method of inferencing is used? Justify your answer. **2**

(ii) Describe **one** disadvantage of using this method of inferencing in this situation. **1**

After the system has been introduced, a holiday maker uses the expert system to select a hotel, but finds it is further from the beach than expected when she arrives in the holiday resort.

(*d*) Name **two** people who could be blamed for the unsuitability and justify your answer. **2**

(8)

Total for Section 3 Part B (25)

[*END OF SECTION 3—PART B*]

[Turn over

Marks

SECTION 3

PART C—The Internet

22. (*a*) Ahmed is creating a website. He is told that there are many different types of *web authoring* packages available. State **two** features of a "web authoring" package he might use when creating the website. **2**

(*b*) Ahmed wants to include photographs on his website. Explain why he might need to use picture compression. **1**

(*c*) Ahmed uses relative page addressing when constructing the site.

Describe what relative page addressing is. **2**

(5)

23. Universities in three different countries communicate ideas and research data using various Internet services.

(*a*) Which Internet service would provide them with real time picture and sound communication? **1**

(*b*) Which service would they use to upload data files directly to another computer? **1**

(*c*) They wish to speed up the transfer rate when uploading the files. Describe **two** communications hardware components they could upgrade. **2**

(*d*) One university suggests they could exchange files using the Internet newsgroup service. Suggest **one** reason why a newsgroup would not be a suitable way of exchanging their research files. **1**

(5)

24. Varga is an isolated island in the North Sea. The inhabitants rely heavily on the Internet to keep in touch with people on the mainland.

(*a*) Many inhabitants use the Internet to work from home. Describe **two** social advantages of working in this way. **2**

(*b*) Many of the islanders are *knowledge workers*.

(i) What is a "knowledge worker"? **1**

(ii) Why is this a suitable occupation for island workers? **1**

(*c*) The Computer Misuse Act is applicable on the island. Describe **one** activity the Act is designed to protect. **1**

(5)

25. Visitors to a university computing department are curious about how the Internet works.

(*a*) They discover that data is transmitted using *packets*. Describe what a "packet" is and how packets are used to transmit data. **2**

(*b*) The destination of each packet is determined by an *IP address*. What is an "IP address"? **1**

(*c*) Computers use various protocols like TCP/IP to send data. Name **two** other protocols used to transmit data on the Internet. **2**

(5)

Marks

26. (*a*) Melissa is searching the Internet for information about Korea using a *search engine*. Describe how a "search engine" allows her to find information more quickly. **1**

(*b*) Melissa is looking for information on forests in Korea. Suggest a search which will help her find exactly what she is looking for. **1**

(*c*) She finds a useful site. What feature of her web browser software can she use to store the location of the page for future reference? **1**

(*d*) Melissa discovers that there are computer viruses and new ones appear regularly. Describe how she can avoid computer viruses affecting her computer. **2**

(5)

Total for Section 3 Part C (25)

[*END OF SECTION 3—PART C*]

[*END OF QUESTION PAPER*]

[BLANK PAGE]

INTERMEDIATE 2

2007

[BLANK PAGE]

X216/201

NATIONAL QUALIFICATIONS 2007

THURSDAY, 24 MAY
9.00 AM – 10.30 AM

INFORMATION SYSTEMS
INTERMEDIATE 2

Attempt Sections 1 and 2 and **one part** of Section 3.

Sections 1 and 2 — Attempt all questions within these sections.

Section 3 — This section has three parts:

Part A—Applied Multimedia

Part B—Expert Systems

Part C—The Internet

Choose **one** part of this section and attempt all of the questions within that part.

Read all questions carefully.

Write your answers in the answer book provided. Do not write on the question paper.

Write as neatly as possible.

SCOTTISH QUALIFICATIONS AUTHORITY

SECTION 1

Marks

Attempt all questions in this section.

1. What is an entity in a relational database? 1

2. A database has a field of type *link*.

Give an example of what might be found in this type of field. 1

3. A car showroom keeps information about vehicles it has to sell in a database. Part of the database has been sorted as shown below.

Make	**Model**	**Year of Registration**	**Mileage**
Renoir	Chloe	2001	37564
Pursio	205	2001	36542
Jokeswagon	Tennis	2001	35004
Renoir	Magritte	2002	45089
Renoir	Chloe	2002	24659
Missan	Nicra	2004	15487

Describe how the list has been sorted. 2

4. An employee is entering data into a database but misses out one of the fields. As a consequence this message appears on the screen: "The field called 'reference number' cannot be left empty. A value must be typed into this field".

Explain why this message appeared. 1

5. A company rents out cottages to holidaymakers. The list of cottages is updated regularly. For each booking the total cost is calculated and is printed in alphabetical order.

Name	Location	Rental Price	Weeks booked	Total Cost
Forrest View	Woodtown	£350	1	£350
Seaview Cottage	Brightpool	£450	2	£900
Shore Cottage	Blackon	£400	2	£800
TreeTops	Woodtown	£300	3	£900

You are asked to create the list using either word processing or spreadsheet software.

Which application type is more suitable for this job?

Justify your choice. 2

Marks

6. State **one** action an employer could take to reduce the risk of repetitive strain injury (RSI) for employees. **1**

7. (*a*) What is meant by *information intellectual property rights*? **1**

(*b*) Why is it important to safeguard such rights? **1**

8. A hacker illegally accesses a bank computer system and transfers money out of some accounts. Which Act does this breach? **1**

9. A travel agency closes its High Street shops and sells its holidays via its website.

(*a*) State **one** economic implication of this for the company. **1**

(*b*) State **one** economic implication for employees. **1**

10. Shoppers are asked to register on a website before purchasing goods. Here is part of the data input form used to gather information about each shopper.

Forename ______________ Surname ______________

Tick box if you wish to be added to our mailing list ☐

Date of Birth ☐ ☐ / ☐ ☐ / ☐ ☐

Suggest the most suitable data type for the following fields.

(*a*) Mailing list **1**

(*b*) Date of Birth **1**

Total for Section 1 (15)

[*END OF SECTION 1*]

[Turn over

Marks

SECTION 2

Attempt all questions in this section.

11. The *efficiency* of an Information System is determined by the *speed*, *accuracy* and *volume* of the data that is processed.

(*a*) What is meant by "volume" of information? 1

(*b*) Describe the role of a *knowledge worker*. 2

(*c*) State **one** example of a "knowledge worker". 1

(4)

12. An estate agency buys and sells property. It has a website to advertise the properties and networked computers in its main office to manage its information system. The network is connected to a centralised database.

(*a*) What type of applications software should be used to

(i) create the website? 1

(ii) view the website? 1

(*b*) The estate agency has put in place a *network strategy* and a *security strategy*.

(i) State **two** reasons why the estate agency needs to have a "security strategy". 2

(ii) State **two** other strategies that the estate agency would be advised to put in place. 2

(*c*) The data is held on one central computer. State **three** advantages of having a centralised database. 3

(9)

13. (*a*) Explain **two** benefits of an electronic database compared with a manual database. 2

(*b*) Explain what is meant by the term *data modelling*. 2

(*c*) What is meant by a single valued field? 1

It is very common to find duplication of data in a flat file database. This can lead to data becoming inconsistent.

(*d*) (i) What type of database should be used to reduce duplication of data and inconsistency? 1

(ii) State **one** way in which it reduces duplication. 1

(7)

Marks

14. The table below shows an extract from a flat file database about sports.

Instructor and Class

Instructor ID	Instructor Name	ClassCode	SportClass	Level	CostPerclass
JS72	John Smith	JAV1	Javelin	1	£32
		SP1	Sprint	1	£32
		HD1	Hurdles	1	£34
MH82	Mary Hughes	LJ1	Long Jump	1	£28
		SP2	Sprint	2	£25
		TJ1	Triple Jump	1	£25
JG92	John Grant	HD2	Hurdles	2	£38
		JAV2	Javelin	2	£38
		HJ1	High Jump	1	£38

(*a*) (i) Normalise the above table by removing the multi-valued fields, and show how it would be represented in two tables. Identify the Primary keys and Foreign key in the new tables. **7**

(ii) State the purpose of a *key* in a table. **1**

(*b*) State what the relationship is between the tables. **2**

(10)

Total for Section 2 (30)

[*END OF SECTION 2*]

[Turn over

SECTION 3

Marks

PART A—Applied Multimedia

15. A local museum plans to provide an electronic public information point. It will provide information about the museum and its displays.

(*a*) (i) Recommend an appropriate delivery medium for the museum to use in this situation. **1**

(ii) State **two** reasons why this could be the preferred choice of delivery by the museum. **2**

(*b*) What input device would be most suitable for members of the public to use to access the information about the museum? **1**

(*c*) The company constructing the multimedia application have to take account of more than the delivery media.

State **two** other aspects that make up the analysis stage of development and state a reason for the inclusion of **each** aspect. **4**

(*d*) The application includes audio files. Describe **two** methods by which the size of the files could be reduced. **2**

(10)

16. A business multimedia application allows users to navigate from any screen directly to any other screen.

(*a*) Which type of navigation structure would be most appropriate for this application? **1**

Part of the application allows users to enter their personal details to be sent further information about products.

(*b*) Which piece of legislation protects users' details submitted in this way? **1**

(*c*) (i) Which type of user interface should the designer use to allow submission of users' details? **1**

(ii) Give a reason for your answer. **1**

(*d*) State **two** techniques that can be used to navigate through a multimedia application. **2**

(*e*) The text in the application included a number of *lists*. State **two** other means by which text may be clearly displayed. **2**

(8)

Marks

17. A company is producing a multimedia application for children. They wish to include cartoon characters from popular TV shows.

(*a*) The graphic designer is worried about the inclusion of these characters.

Explain why she should be worried about including these characters. **1**

(*b*) Some illustrations will be cartoon drawings and others will be full colour photographs. All the illustrations will require editing and manipulating. The designer has graphics software that can create *bitmapped* or *vector* graphics.

Which type of graphics software should be used for

(i) the cartoon drawings? **1**

(ii) the full colour photographs? **1**

(*c*) The application includes over 1,500 photographs. The graphic designer has been instructed to reduce the overall storage requirements for these photographs. Describe **two** methods by which this could be done. **2**

(*d*) Once the application has been completed, extensive testing is carried out. Explain the purpose of:

(i) screen tests; **1**

(ii) navigation tests. **1**

(7)

Total for Section 3 Part A (25)

[*END OF SECTION 3—PART A*]

[Turn over

SECTION 3

Marks

PART B—Expert Systems

18. The diagram below shows how a user interacts with an expert system.

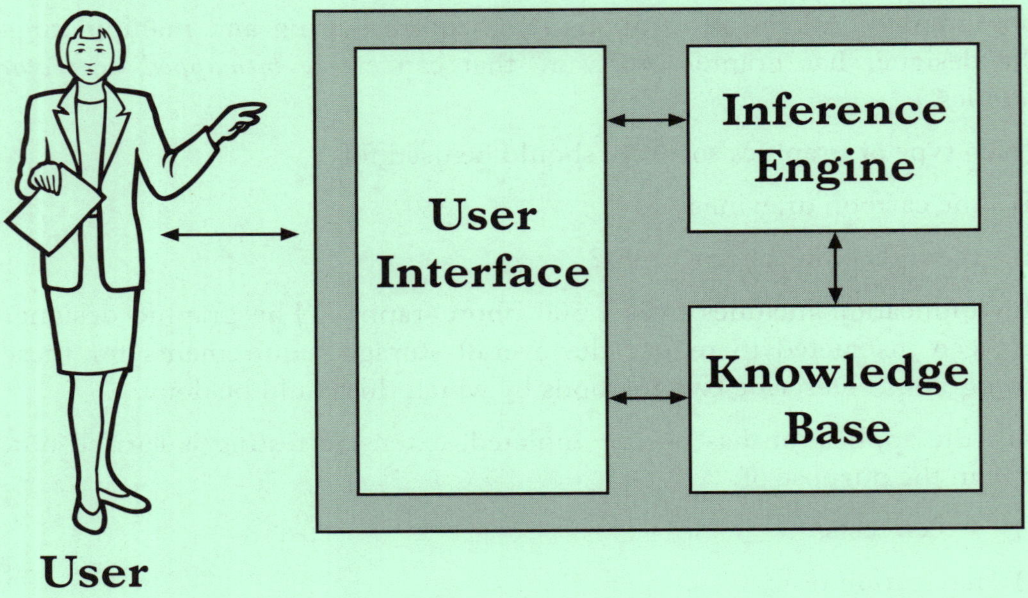

(*a*) State **one** purpose of an expert system. **1**

(*b*) Describe the main features of the following components:

(i) Knowledge Base **1**

(ii) Inference Engine **1**

(*c*) The User Interface is used to display questions to the user and obtain answers. It is also used to display advice and justification.

Describe **two** features used to evaluate the quality of the user interface. **2**

(*d*) Describe **two** justification facilities which would be available in an expert system. **2**

(7)

19. A nature reserve currently provides information sheets to visitors to help them identify butterflies they can see around the nature reserve.

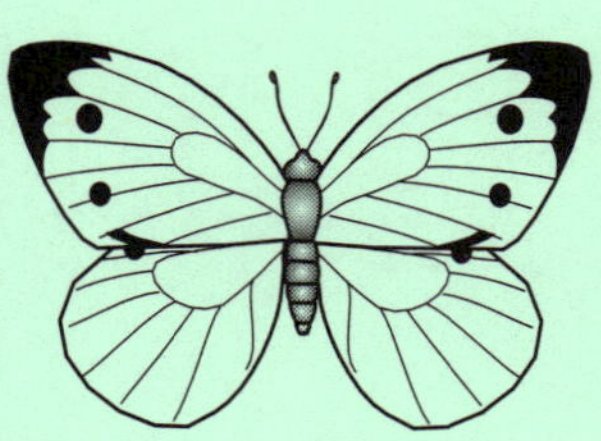

An expert system is being introduced into the visitor centre to replace the information sheets.

(*a*) What category of expert system would the nature reserve use to identify the butterflies? **1**

Many people are involved in developing the expert system for the nature reserve.

(*b*) Explain the roles of the following personnel in this situation:

(i) domain expert **1**

(ii) knowledge engineer **1**

Marks

19. (continued)

(*c*) Part of the knowledge is represented in a decision tree.

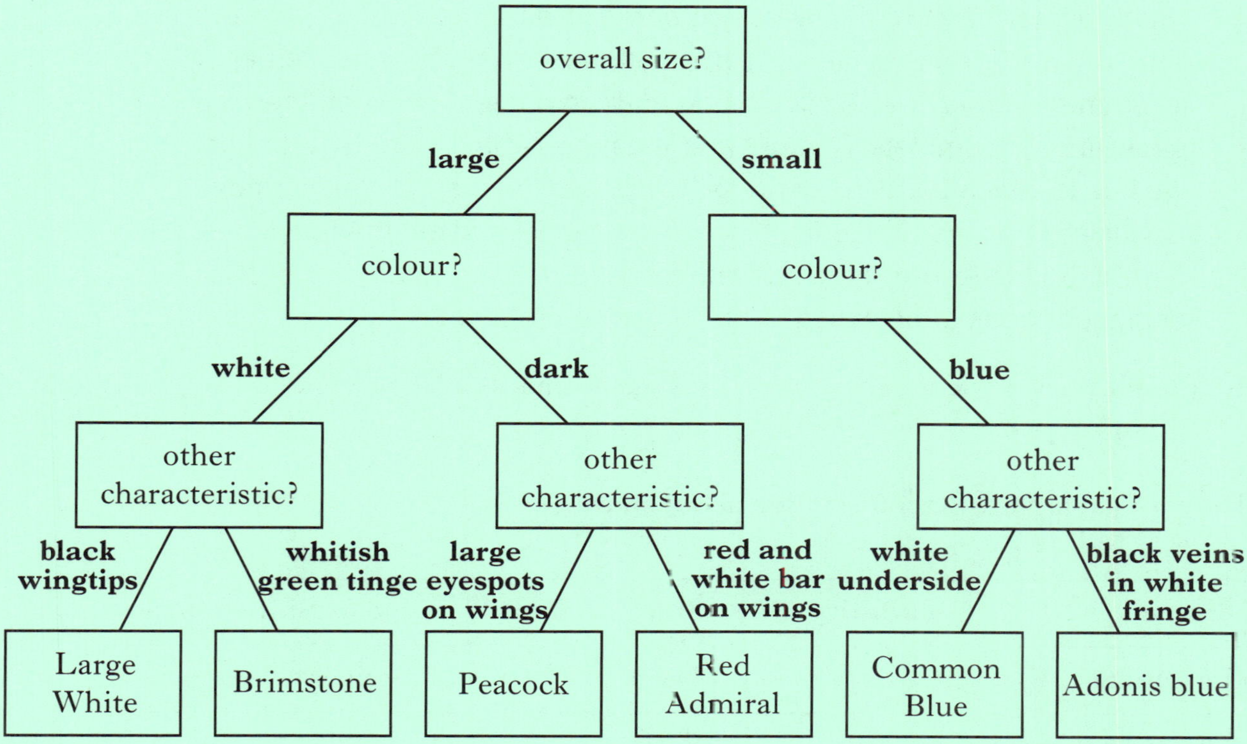

This is used to write the following production rule.

IF	overall size IS large
AND	colour IS white
AND	other characteristic IS black wingtips
THEN	butterfly type IS large white

(i) Design production rules for **two** other types of butterflies using the information in the decision tree. **4**

(ii) Identify the method of *inferencing* that has been used in the rule above. **1**

(*d*) The final stage of developing the expert system is *system validation.* Describe **one** technique used to carry out "system validation". **1**

(9)

[Turn over

Marks

20. A printer manufacturer wants to develop an expert system to use on their helpdesk to determine the nature of problems with ink jet printers. Here is some of the knowledge to be included in the system.

> "Each printer has two lights—a red one and an amber one. If the red light is flashing and the amber light is off then the problem is the paper is jammed. When the red light is on and the amber light is off then the paper tray is completely empty and must be refilled. The amber light flashes to indicate the ink cartridge is low, while an empty ink cartridge is indicated by the amber light on. In both these cases, the red light is off. If both the red light and amber light are on, then the service engineer needs to be called to attend to the problem."

Represent the knowledge about the printer problems as a factor table. **(5)**

21. Here is a table showing information about snowboards.

Shape	**Flexibility**	**Size**	**Type of Snowboard**
Directional	Soft	Narrow	Freerider
Directional Twin	Very Soft	Wide	Freestyle
Directional	Stiff	Very Narrow	Racing

The information could be put into an expert system or into a database.

(*a*) How many records would be in the database?

(*b*) How many rules would be in the expert system?

(*c*) How many fields would make up each record in the database?

(*d*) How many conditions would each rule have in the expert system? **(4)**

Total for Section 3 Part B (25)

[*END OF SECTION 3—PART B*]

Marks

SECTION 3

PART C—The Internet

22. A family are planning a weekend break and wish to book a hotel room on-line. Their favourite hotel chain is called the Valiant Group which owns hundreds of hotels throughout the UK and abroad. Each hotel has different facilities.

(*a*) They use an Internet search engine to find a Valiant hotel with a swimming pool, anywhere except London. Write down a Boolean search that would produce the required results. **3**

(*b*) When they make their reservation with the hotel their details are stored in a database and they receive a booking reference number.

(i) What piece of legislation protects information stored in this way? **1**

(ii) Why is the booking reference number required? **1**

(*c*) They wish to download a file containing a map showing directions to the hotel. Which protocol will they use? **1**

(*d*) They notice that their browser is showing the *IP address* of the server containing the file. What is an "IP address"? **1**

(*e*) Communication takes place between the family and the hotel by e-mail.

Name the protocols used for:

(i) sending e-mails; **1**

(ii) receiving e-mails. **1**

(9)

23. A multinational company is holding a conference at one of the Valiant hotels.

(*a*) Some people attending the conference have laptop computers but all of the attendees need to access the Internet.

Name **one** other portable device they might use to access the Internet. **1**

(*b*) The attendees communicate with each other using *newsgroups* and *chat*. Describe the difference in communication method between "newsgroups" and "chat". **2**

(*c*) On the second day of the conference, a group of attendees intends to participate in a *video conference* with company employees in Berlin.

(i) What extra piece of hardware would the participants require? **1**

(ii) State **one** advantage to the company and **one** advantage to the employees of using "video conferencing". **2**

(6)

[Turn over for Question 24 on *Page twelve*

Marks

24. The Valiant group has a centralised booking system, and each hotel has its own website.

Helen Pertwee's job is to create, maintain and update each of the hotel websites.

(*a*) She uses web authoring software to create the web pages. The software has a *hyperlink tool*. What is the purpose of the "hyperlink tool"? **1**

(*b*) She has to decide whether the hyperlinks use *absolute page addressing* or *relative page addressing*.

(i) Describe how "absolute page addressing" works. **1**

(ii) Describe **two** advantages of "relative page addressing". **2**

(*c*) Helen finds that her page with a photograph on it takes a long time to load. What could Helen do to the photograph to make it load faster? **1**

(*d*) Each hotel has its own intranet with workstations, a *multiplexer* and a *router*. Through this, guests can access the Internet.

(i) Describe the purpose of a "multiplexer". **1**

(ii) Describe the function of the "router". **2**

(*e*) What must Helen do to keep the computers protected from *viruses*? **2**

(10)

Total for Section 3 Part C (25)

[*END OF SECTION 3—PART C*]

[*END OF QUESTION PAPER*]

INTERMEDIATE 2

2008

[BLANK PAGE]

X216/201

NATIONAL QUALIFICATIONS 2008

MONDAY, 19 MAY
9.00 AM – 10.30 AM

INFORMATION SYSTEMS
INTERMEDIATE 2

Attempt Section I and Section II and **one** Part of Section III.

Section I – Attempt all questions.

Section II – Attempt all questions.

Section III – This section has three parts:

Part A – Applied Multimedia

Part B – Expert Systems

Part C – The Internet

Choose **one** part and answer **all** of the questions in that part.

Read each question carefully.

Write your answers in the answer book provided. **Do not** write on the question paper.

Write as neatly as possible.

Answer in sentences wherever possible.

Marks

SECTION I

Attempt all questions in this section.

1. What type of application software would you recommend to allow users to communicate across the Internet in real-time? 1

2. Here is the design for a pupil database.

Field Name	Data Type	Sample Data
Forename	text	Lidia
Surname	text	Witkiewicz
Class	text	4B
Subjects	text	English, Computing, Gaelic, Art

State the term used to describe text fields such as *Subjects*. 1

3. State **two** offences covered by the Computer Misuse Act 1990. 2

4. What is *on-line* help? 1

5. Name the object in a spreadsheet that contains a single piece of text, a number or a formula. 1

6. State **one** security method that may be used by an organisation to ensure a hacker cannot access data. 1

Marks

7.

> When travelling to a foreign country it is important to have a passport with you. A passport is a document that identifies you as a citizen of the country that issues the passport.
>
> At an airport or ferry port there is usually someone inspecting passports, and they will use an ink stamp to mark your passport, showing that you have entered a new country.

The diagram above shows a small part of a word processed document.

(*a*) Identify **one** data object from the text above. **1**

(*b*) Name **one** operation that could be performed on this data object. **1**

8. Data has to be gathered and stored before it can be processed.

State **two** electronic methods that allow large amounts of data to be gathered. **2**

9. State **two** advantages of purchasing music on-line. **2**

10. Explain why typing an e-mail message in capitals is seen as poor *netiquette*. **1**

11. A piece of computer software offers users menus and keyboard commands to perform various tasks. Explain why the software offers users these different types of HCI. **1**

Total for Section I (15)

[*END OF SECTION I*]

[Turn over

Marks

SECTION II

Attempt all questions in this section.

12. (*a*) A database is a collection of related information about people or objects. Many databases use manual data storage.

State **three** problems that are associated with manual databases. **3**

(*b*) State **one** advantage of an electronic database over a manual system. **1**

(*c*) Two types of computerised database are *flat file* and *relational*.

(i) What is meant by a "flat file" database? **1**

(ii) State **two** limitations of a "flat file" database. **2**

(*d*) *Normalisation* is a process used when a relational database is being designed.

State **three** reasons why "normalisation" is required when using a relational model. **3**

(10)

13. The data cards below show part of the database used by a music teacher to keep track of pupils and the instruments they are given.

Pupil ID 023
First Name John
Second Name Murnie

Reference No.	Musical Instrument	Make
G78	Guitar	Fenbar
D34	Drums	Gudwig

Pupil ID 058
First Name Shuna
Second Name Ali

Reference No.	Musical Instrument	Make
C18	Clarinet	Boyd
R12	Recorder	Sprat

(*a*) (i) Normalise the data shown above by removing the multi-value fields. Identify the Primary and Foreign keys. **7**

(ii) State the relationship between the entities created in (*a*)(i). **1**

(*b*) When the database is implemented, the content of the field *Musical Instrument* is limited to certain values.

Name this validation check. **1**

(*c*) When the database is implemented, suggest the most suitable field type for *Reference No.* **1**

(10)

Marks

14. Apple Bay High School has a policy of healthy eating in the school. The school student council wants to publicise the policy.

The student council are to produce a special healthy eating information brochure containing pictures, alongside recipes and nutritional advice.

(*a*) (i) What type of application software would be most suitable for this purpose? **1**

(ii) State **two** reasons for your answer. **2**

(*b*) The student council wants to include a picture of the student who won the "best recipe" competition.

What will they have to do before they are allowed to include the picture in the brochure? **1**

(*c*) The school has a database of all the people who received a copy of the brochure. A local health club requests a copy of the database. Why should the school not supply the database to the health club? **1**

(*d*) The student council wants to promote their healthy eating policy by creating a website.

(i) What type of application software should be used to construct the website? **1**

(ii) State **two** advantages to the student council of using a website instead of the brochure. **2**

(*e*) Some of the families associated with Apple Bay High School are described as being *information poor*.

(i) Explain what is meant by "information poor". **1**

(ii) State **one** disadvantage that arises from this. **1**

(10)

Total for Section II (30)

[*END OF SECTION II*]

[Turn over

SECTION III

Attempt ONE part of Section III

Part A	**Applied Multimedia**	**Page 7**	**Questions 15 to 16**
Part B	**Expert Systems**	**Page 9**	**Questions 17 to 19**
Part C	**The Internet**	**Page 11**	**Questions 20 to 22**

Choose **one** part and answer **all** of the questions in that part.

Marks

SECTION III

PART A—Applied Multimedia

Attempt ALL questions in this section.

15. A low cost air travel company wishes to update its website. This new website will be the only method customers have to book flights.

(*a*) Suggest **two** reasons why the company is using the website as the only method of booking flights. **2**

(*b*) When booking a flight, the customer sees the following screen.

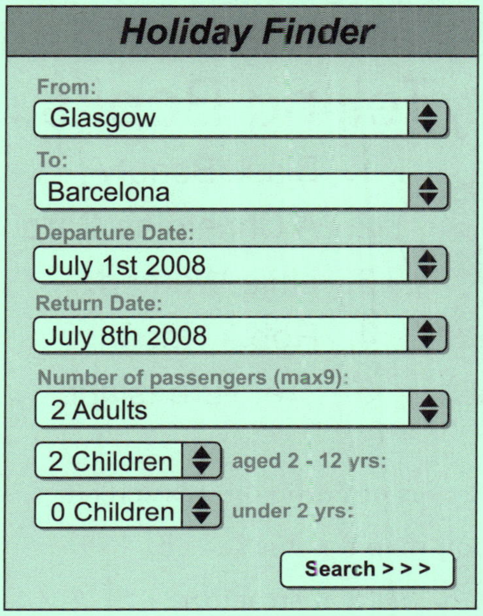

(i) State the type of search facility shown above. **1**

(ii) State the type of user interface being used above. **1**

(iii) State **one** reason why this type of interface has been chosen. **1**

(*c*) Once the flights have been chosen, the customer will need to supply their personal details. Which type of user interface would you suggest for this Web page? **1**

(*d*) State the job title of the specialist who creates the Web pages for customers to use. **1**

(*e*) The company wishes to test the website before it is uploaded to the Internet. A group of customers is asked to test and evaluate the website.

(i) Explain why the pages need to be tested. **1**

(ii) State **one** method of testing the website they might use. **1**

(iii) State the reason why the evaluation would be useful. **1**

(10)

[Turn over

Marks

16. Eryn is an audio media specialist. She is working on a *CAL* storybook project. The project is a multimedia program that combines text and pictures with the audio of the stories being read.

(*a*) (i) What does "CAL" stand for? **1**

(ii) Suggest **one** reason why an audio recording of the story would make this a better program. **1**

(*b*) There is limited storage capacity for Eryn's audio recordings.

Describe **one** method of reducing the storage requirements for the audio recordings. **1**

(*c*) Laura is the project manager. She wishes audio to be added to the main screen.

(i) State **two** possible uses of audio on this screen. **2**

(ii) Draw the navigation map for this screen. **1**

(iii) Name this type of navigation structure. **1**

(iv) State which type of multimedia authoring software you would recommend to create this application. **1**

(v) Give **one** reason for your choice. **1**

(*d*) Each book title has a *link* to a new screen. What is a "link"? **1**

(*e*) A *Transition* occurs when one screen changes to another.

(i) What is a "transition"? **1**

(ii) Explain why a "transition" might be used. **1**

(*f*) Once the program has been completed, various pieces of user documentation are written.

(i) Describe the purpose of user instructions. **1**

(ii) Explain why hardware and software system requirements are important when buying the program. **1**

(*g*) Which piece of legislation covers illegal copying of software? **1**

(15)

Total for Section III Part A (25)

[*END OF SECTION III—PART A—APPLIED MULTIMEDIA*]

Marks

SECTION III

PART B—Expert Systems

Attempt ALL questions in this section.

17. Dovaphone is a mobile phone company that offers several options to its customers who want a monthly contract. Dovaphone is considering implementing an expert system to help customers select the most suitable option for their needs.

(*a*) State the category of the proposed expert system. **1**

(*b*) The first stage of developing an expert system is called *knowledge acquisition.*

State **two** methods used for "knowledge acquisition". **2**

(*c*) Some of the knowledge acquired is represented as the following attribute-value pairs.

Option 1 (minutes=100, text messages=50, WAP bundle=No)
Option 2 (minutes=100, text messages=100, WAP bundle=No)
Option 3 (minutes=100, text messages=100, WAP bundle=Yes)
Option 4 (minutes=200, text messages=100, WAP bundle=No)
Option 5 (minutes=200, text messages=100, WAP bundle=Yes)

(i) Represent the attribute-value pairs as a decision tree. **5**

(ii) Who would be responsible for creating this representation during the development of the expert system? **1**

(9)

18. Dovaphone provides a range of mobile phones in their shops. The details about the features available on each model are currently held in a database. To help a customer select a suitable phone, the salesperson enters the customer's answers to a number of questions about their phone needs into the database system.

The company decides to replace the database system with an expert system.

(*a*) One advantage of an expert system is that it can provide *justification.*

(i) State **two** types of "justification". **2**

(ii) State **two** benefits to the customer of "justification" facilities in this expert system. **2**

(*b*) Compare the output obtained from a database system and an expert system. **2**

(*c*) Describe how the company would test the new expert system. **2**

(8)

[Turn over

Marks

19. Motor racing cars can have 3 different types of tyres—Slicks, Intermediates or Wets—fitted during a race depending on the weather and track conditions.

An expert system is to be used to indicate the most appropriate tyre selection based on a number of criteria.

Here is the factor table showing the knowledge to be entered into an expert system.

Present Weather	Track Condition	Race Duration Forecast	Tyre Selection
Dry	Dry	Dry	Slicks
Dry	Dry	Rain	Slicks
Dry	Standing Water	*	Intermediates
Rain	Dry	Dry	Intermediates
Rain	Dry	Rain	Wets
Rain	Standing Water	*	Wets

Two of the rules have been written below.

IF Present Weather is Dry
AND Track Condition is Standing Water
THEN Tyre Selection is Intermediates.

IF Present Weather is Rain
AND Track Condition is Dry
AND Race Duration Forecast is Dry
THEN Tyre Selection is Intermediates.

(*a*) Write the rules required for Wets. **4**

(*b*) State which component of the expert system is used to store the facts and rules. **1**

(*c*) The two main methods of inferencing used in expert systems that use production rules are *backward chaining* and *forward chaining*.

(i) Describe the difference between these methods of inferencing. **2**

(ii) State which method is used in the tyre selection example. **1**

(8)

Total for Section III Part B (25)

[*END OF SECTION III—PART B—EXPERT SYSTEMS*]

Marks

SECTION III

PART C—The Internet

Attempt ALL questions in this section.

20. This diagram represents part of the network in a school.

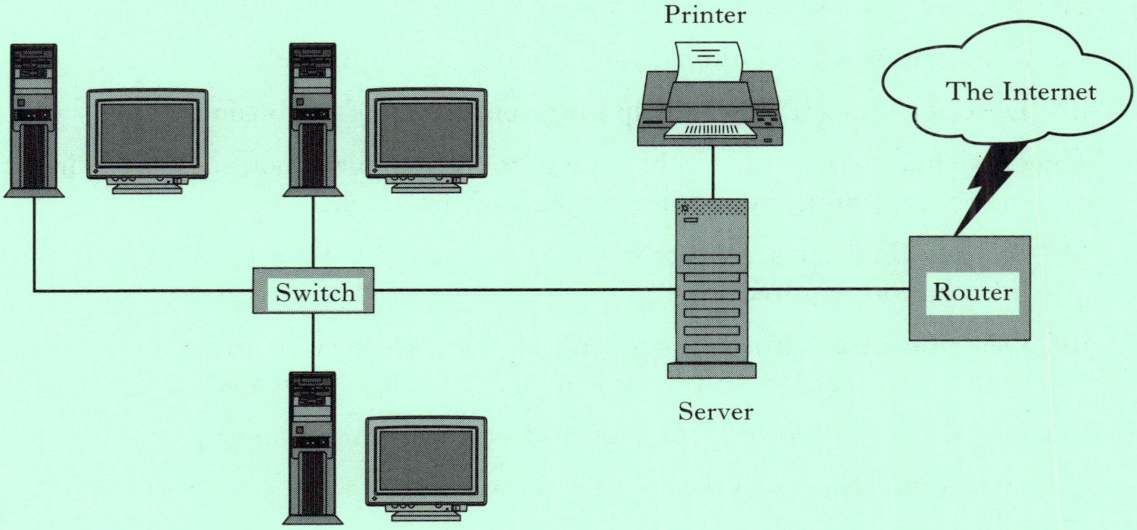

(*a*) (i) State the purpose of the router. **1**

(ii) State the purpose of the switch. **1**

(*b*) The school has implemented a *backup strategy*.

Why does the school need a "backup strategy"? **1**

(*c*) The school's Internet connection has recently had an increase in bandwidth.

Describe **one** way pupils may notice the increase in bandwidth when using the Internet. **1**

(4)

[Turn over

Marks

21. Sameer runs a company selling second hand books.

He has registered with an Internet Service Provider and now has access to the World Wide Web and an e-mail account.

(*a*) State **two** types of application software he could use to access his e-mail. **2**

(*b*) Sameer intends to use his e-mail account to help run his business.

(i) State **one** way he could use e-mail for business purposes. **1**

(ii) Describe how this would help in the efficiency of his business. **1**

(*c*) Sameer wants to use a search engine to find news about auctions in Scotland, but is not interested in auctions in Edinburgh.

(i) State a Boolean search that could be used by Sameer to find the information required. **2**

(ii) Describe **one** feature of an advanced search service that would be useful to Sameer to find the specific information he wanted. **2**

(*d*) Sameer is using the World Wide Web and e-mail for his business.

Name **two** other Internet services that he might use. **2**

(*e*) As Sameer travels around the country visiting book auctions, he can access the Web and his e-mail using devices other than his computer.

State **one** other device he could use to obtain Internet access. **1**

(11)

Marks

22. Ally is creating a website for Holibobs, a company that sells holidays to its on-line customers.

(*a*) Ally scans photographs of holiday locations from a book so they can be included on the website.

Ally uses *picture compression*.

(i) What is "picture compression"? **1**

(ii) Explain why "picture compression" is required in this situation. **2**

(*b*) Ally creates this Web page.

Name the legislation Ally must comply with to include the images on the website. **1**

(*c*) Ally used Web authoring software to create the Web page. One of the features of the software was the *hyperlink tool*.

(i) State the purpose of the "hyperlink tool". **1**

(ii) Describe how Ally used this tool in the Web page shown. **1**

(*d*) The address of this Web page is http://www.holibob.co.uk/index.htm. It uses the *http protocol*. Ally creates a folder in the same directory as the index page to store all the graphics for the Web page. The folder is called *images*. The graphic used for Scotland has the filename **edinburgh.jpg**.

(i) What is a "protocol"? **1**

(ii) What is the purpose of the "http"? **1**

(iii) Using absolute addressing, write down the address of the graphic used for Scotland. **2**

(10)

Total for Section III Part C (25)

[*END OF SECTION III—PART C—THE INTERNET*]

[*END OF QUESTION PAPER*]

[BLANK PAGE]

INTERMEDIATE 2

2009

[BLANK PAGE]

X216/201

NATIONAL QUALIFICATIONS 2009

FRIDAY, 29 MAY
9.00 AM – 10.30 AM

INFORMATION SYSTEMS
INTERMEDIATE 2

Attempt Section I and Section II and **one** Part of Section III.

Section I – Attempt all questions.

Section II – Attempt all questions.

Section III – This section has three parts:

Part A – Applied Multimedia

Part B – Expert Systems

Part C – The Internet

Choose **one** part and answer **all** of the questions in that part.

Read each question carefully.

Write your answers in the answer book provided. **Do not** write on the question paper.

Write as neatly as possible.

Answer in sentences wherever possible.

Marks

SECTION I

Attempt all questions in this section.

1. Describe **one** difference between *data* and *information*. **1**

2. The spreadsheet below shows the sales figures for a concert.

	A	B	C	D
1	Kinto Katz Ticket Sales			
2		Quantity	Price	Value
3	Front Seating	150	£11.00	£1,650.00
4	Rear Seating	150	£12.00	£1,800.00
5	Upper Seating	200	£10.00	£2,000.00
6	Standing	500	£7.50	£3,750.00
7			Total	£9,200.00

(*a*) State **one** *data object* used in a spreadsheet. **1**

(*b*) From the spreadsheet above, identify **one** *formatting function* that has been carried out. **1**

3. A travel agent allows customers to book holidays online.

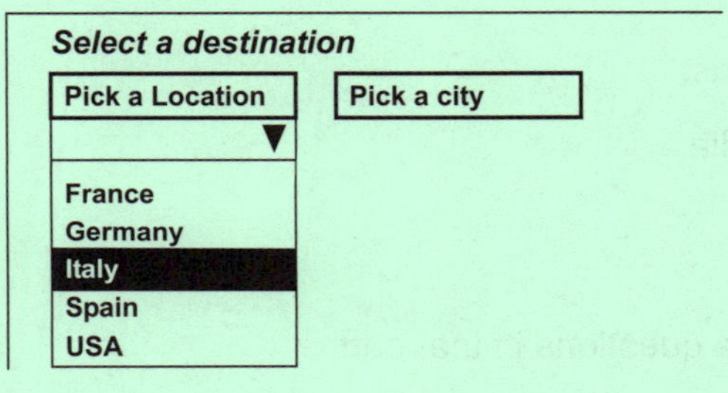

State the type of *validation* used to ensure that customers only choose holidays in countries offered by the travel agent. **1**

4. Slideshows and brochures are used to advertise products.

(*a*) Name the type of application software used to produce a slideshow. **1**

(*b*) Name the type of application software used to produce a brochure. **1**

5. State **two** reasons why a company may need to have a network strategy. **2**

6. State **one** advantage of using linked tables in a relational database rather than a flat file database. **1**

Marks

7. The database below shows some of the results of runners taking part in the Olympic Fun Run.

No	Start	Finish	Forename	Surname	Gender (M/F)	Athletics Club
1011	10:15:00	11:12:17	Eric	Gallimore	M	www.olympicharriers.com
1475	10:15:00	11:15:33	Daniel	McHugh	M	www.olympicrunners.co.uk
2232	10:20:00	11:41:12	Vicky	Chen	F	www.ba-athleticsclub.co.uk
2246	10:20:00	11:20:04	Jembu	Malf	M	www.runforfun.org.uk

(*a*) Suggest the most appropriate field type for the Start field. **1**

(*b*) Suggest the most appropriate field type for the Athletics Club field. **1**

8. Give **one** example of how the use of technology has changed the way people shop. **1**

9. The school information system shown below is used to print out a list of absentees.

ID Number	Forename	Surname	Class
20081237	Alison	Begley	1A
20081348	Anna	Smith	1A
20081872	Mirza	Hanif	1B
20081903	Patrick	McCann	1B
20082760	Charlie	McKenzie	1B
20081845	Naiem	Mohammed	1C
20082856	Eilidh	Fraser	1D
20081992	Johann	Schmidt	1D

(*a*) Describe how the above list has been sorted. **2**

(*b*) State **one** advantage of using an electronic information system rather than a manual system. **1**

Total for Section I (15)

[*END OF SECTION I*]

[Turn over

Marks

SECTION II

Attempt all questions in this section.

10. PawsHome is a company with cat homes across Scotland. It stores information about its cat homes and employees on paper. A sample of the data held is shown below.

<table>
<tr><th>Employee Name</th><th>Gender</th><th>Age</th><th>Position</th><th>Employee No</th><th>Cat Home</th><th>City</th></tr>
<tr><td>Peter Jones</td><td>Male</td><td>34</td><td>Manager</td><td>134</td><td rowspan="2">HOM23</td><td rowspan="2">Perth</td></tr>
<tr><td>Li Chan</td><td>Female</td><td>43</td><td>Secretary</td><td>145</td></tr>
<tr><td>Mary Smith</td><td>Female</td><td>29</td><td>Manager</td><td>234</td><td rowspan="2">HOM45</td><td rowspan="2">Inverness</td></tr>
<tr><td>Amadi Adumatta</td><td>Male</td><td>52</td><td>Secretary</td><td>265</td></tr>
<tr><td>Lisa Smith</td><td>Female</td><td>35</td><td>Cleaner</td><td>233</td><td rowspan="2">HOM19</td><td rowspan="2">Perth</td></tr>
<tr><td>Peter Jones</td><td>Male</td><td>36</td><td>Supervisor</td><td>237</td></tr>
</table>

(*a*) Before the database can be implemented, the data must be normalised.

(i) Explain why the Employee Name attribute would **not** be suitable as a primary key. **1**

(ii) Normalise the above table by removing the multi-valued fields, and show how it would be represented in two tables. Clearly indicate meaningful table names and the primary and foreign keys. **7**

(iii) State the one to many relationship between the above tables. **1**

(*b*) State the type of validation check that should be used to ensure that the Age attribute cannot be left empty. **1**

(*c*) PawsHome must comply with the Data Protection Act.

(i) In terms of the Data Protection Act, state what PawsHome must do before they store personal data. **1**

(ii) Who is the data controller in this case? **1**

(12)

Marks

11. John runs a car rental dealership. He has created a database and started entering data into it. The database is shown below.

Reg No	Make	Model	Engine Size (cc)	Daily Rental (£)
DCT04FT	Alpha	Siesta	1400	15
DCS04SJ	Alpha	Spring	1800	25
AEF54JY	Epsilon	Dash	1400	20
PFD53GF	Delta	Tiger	1400	20
EEE51EG	Sigma	Vector	1600	25
KTH50JJ	Alpha	Focus	1800	15

(*a*) A customer phones asking for a particular type of car. John used the database to output the following results.

Reg No	Make	Model	Engine Size (cc)	Daily Rental (£)
DCS04SJ	Alpha	Spring	1800	25
KTH50JJ	Alpha	Focus	1800	15

(i) Describe how John queried the database to get the results shown above. **3**

(ii) What name is given to the printed output from a database? **1**

(*b*) Reg No could be used as a *primary key*. What is the purpose of a "primary key"? **1**

(*c*) When creating a database, John noticed that he could add an *object* type field.

State **one** type of information that would be stored in an "object" type field. **1**

(*d*) Describe the purpose of the database user interface. **1**

(7)

[Turn over

Marks

12. Blush sells cosmetics in their High Street shops.

(*a*) Blush employs several *knowledge workers*.

Describe the job of a "knowledge worker". **1**

(*b*) Blush has a centralised database situated at its head office.

(i) What is meant by a centralised database? **1**

(ii) At the end of each day, Blush's information system is used to total that day's sales and to save the results on the hard disk.

State the **two** functions of this information system that are being carried out at the end of each day. **2**

(*c*) Angelique has just joined Blush from another cosmetics company.

(i) Angelique brought a copy of her previous employer's test results for a new lip gloss.

State **one** of the ethical implications of Blush using these test results. **1**

(ii) Before Angelique could start work, she had to sign Blush's *netiquette* agreement form.

Describe **two** rules you would expect to find on Blush's "netiquette" form. **2**

(iii) Angelique uses a computer program that contains a series of tasks that teach her how to use Blush's database software.

Name this type of program. **1**

(*d*) Ken is a website developer for Blush who has recently created Blush's cosmetic online shop.

(i) Name the type of software that would be most appropriate to build and maintain a complex website. **1**

(ii) With the introduction of the online shop, Blush found that their sales had increased significantly due to new customers.

Give one example of how Blush may have gained new customers through the online shop. **1**

(iii) Ken has found that a former employee has been hacking into Blush's computer system.

State the law that the former employee has broken. **1**

(11)

Total for Section II (30)

[*END OF SECTION II*]

SECTION III

Attempt ONE part of Section III

Choose **one** part and answer **all** of the questions in that part.

[Turn over

Marks

SECTION III

PART A—Applied Multimedia

Attempt ALL questions in this section.

13. A museum has decided to create interactive multimedia information points around the museum.

(*a*) Below is part of the report from the analysis stage

> *. . . the information points should allow visitors (targeted 8–14 year old children and their parents) to be able to see and hear the information about the exhibits without distracting other visitors around them. The refurbishment of the museum will be completed by November of this year and the information points must be created, tested and in place by then. The museum can afford to spend £15 000 on the development of the information points . . .*

(i) The report on the analysis stage contains the purpose and budget available for the multimedia development. State **two** other aspects that have been considered in the above analysis report. **2**

(ii) Recommend the most appropriate delivery medium for the museum to use in this situation. **1**

(*b*) One of the screen designs for the presentation is shown below.

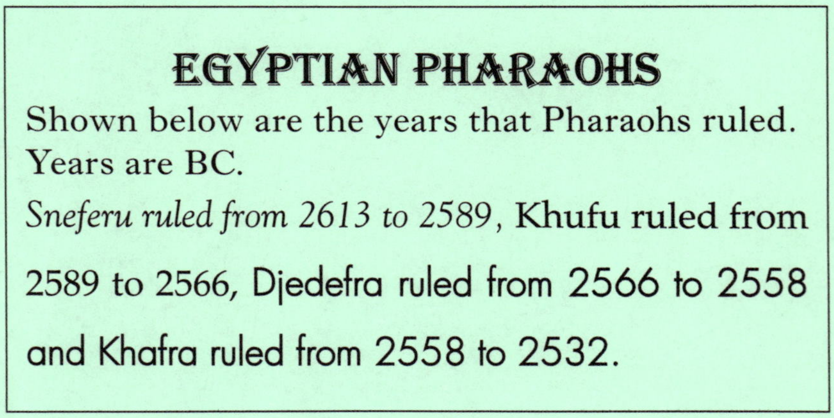

State **two** text design principles that have been broken in the creation of the above design. **2**

Marks

13. (continued)

(*c*) One of the screens from the museum information point is shown below.

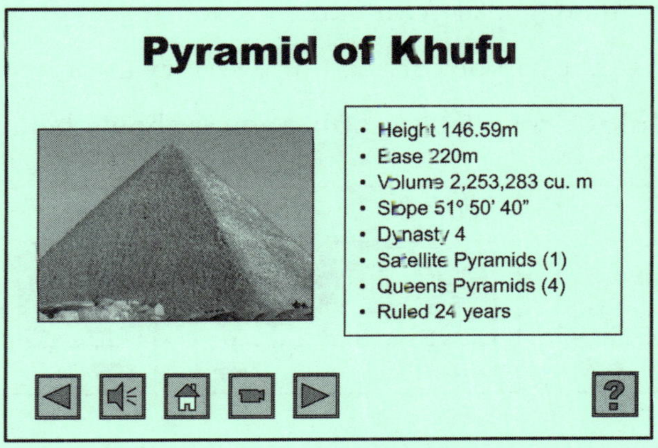

(i) State the type of user interface being used above. **1**

(ii) This type of interface was chosen because of its ease of use.

State **one** reason why the interface shown above is easy to use. **1**

(*d*) During the testing stage, a *navigation test* was carried out.

Explain the purpose of a "navigation test". **1**

(*e*) The museum evaluates the multimedia application in terms of *fitness for purpose*.

Describe **one** method the museum could use to evaluate "fitness for purpose". **1**

(*f*) The completed multimedia application plays background music.

(i) The background music was captured by sampling. Explain how the sampling rate affects the quality of the audio. **1**

(ii) Describe **one** benefit of providing background music. **1**

(*g*) During the evaluation process, many museum staff complained that the background music can be repetitive and distracts them from their jobs.

(i) Describe a **software** solution to the above problem. **1**

(ii) Describe a **hardware** solution to the above problem. **1**

(*h*) If visitors to the museum are unsure how to use the multimedia application they can click on the ? button and the screen shown opposite appears.

State the name given to this type of screen. **1**

(14)

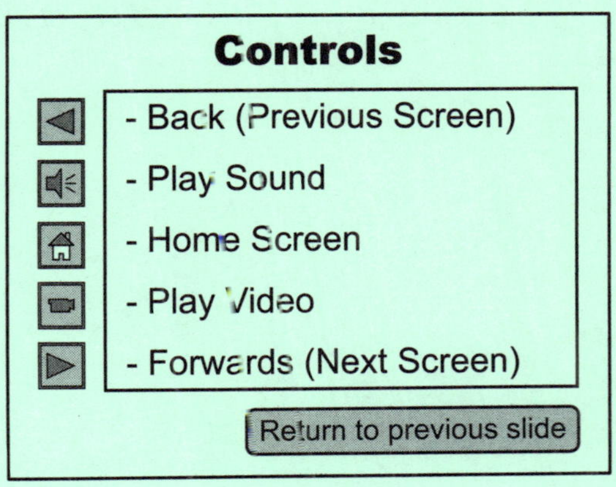

Marks

14. MultiCorp develops multimedia applications for business.

(*a*) State **two** examples of multimedia use for business. 2

(*b*) Mary is the project manager of MultiCorps's development team.

Describe **two** tasks that will be carried out by Mary as project manager. 2

(*c*) The design for MultiCorps's latest application is shown below.

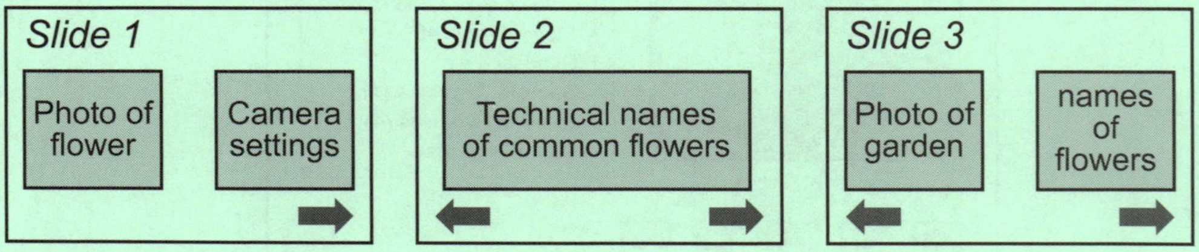

(i) State the type of navigation structure that would be most appropriate in this case. 1

(ii) State the type of software you would recommend MultiCorp use for this project. 1

(iii) State the job title of the person who would provide the technical knowledge that is required for the creation of slide two. 1

(*d*) MultiCorp's project includes 700 colour photographs which take up 6·5 gigabytes of storage. The graphic artist has been instructed to reduce the storage requirements for the photographs from 6·5 gigabytes to 3 gigabytes.

(i) Describe **two** methods of reducing the storage required for the photographs. 2

(ii) Name the storage medium that would be best suited for distributing the project to customers. 1

(iii) Some of the photographs have been copied from a website.

Which law may have been broken? 1

(11)

Total for Section III Part A (25)

[*END OF SECTION III—PART A—APPLIED MULTIMEDIA*]

Marks

SECTION III

PART B—Expert Systems

Attempt ALL questions in this section.

15. A new expert system is being developed for a travel company, to advise tourists on suitable types of holidays.

(*a*) One stage of the expert system development cycle is *knowledge representation.*

(i) State the personnel involved at the "knowledge representation" stage. 1

(ii) State **one** technique used at the "knowledge representation" stage. 1

(*b*) The diagram below shows a screen from the initial version of the expert system.

> Q: Do you want a high activity holiday? [Why?]
>
> **User response: yes**
>
> Q: Do you want a beach location? [Why?]
>
> **User response: yes**
>
> Advice: You should choose a water sports holiday.
>
> [Explain]

(i) The *inference engine* is one component of an expert system.

Identify one element shown above which was **generated** by the "inference engine". 1

(ii) State which component of the expert system is responsible for **displaying** "Q: Do you want a beach location?" 1

(iii) State which component of the expert system would be altered when a new type of holiday is added. 1

(iv) Describe the purpose of the "Explain" button on the screen. 1

(v) Describe the purpose of the "Why?" button on the screen. 1

(*c*) Describe **two** economic implications for the travel company of introducing the holiday expert system. 2

(*d*) Another expert system is being developed. This will list holiday items that should be packed. It will also provide a set of steps to follow so that tourists are organised. State the category of this expert system. 1

(*e*) Describe how querying an expert system would differ from querying a database. 2

(12)

Marks

16. A digital television company offers four packages to their customers, each with a different range of channels—Basic, Bronze, Silver and Gold.
The Basic package includes 15 TV channels. The Gold package allows the customer to add three more "options" to their package. The Silver package allows a choice of two out of three "options" to be added, while Bronze allows only one "option" to be added.

Shown below is **part** of the factor table showing knowledge to be entered into the expert system.

Sports Option	Movies Option	Kids Option	Package
Yes	Yes	Yes	Gold
Yes	Yes	No	Silver
Yes	No	Yes	Silver
No	Yes	Yes	Silver

(*a*) Complete the factor table using the knowledge available. **4**

(*b*) Write a rule to represent the "Gold" package from the knowledge in the table. **3**

(7)

17. Pat suffers from very painful joints, especially in his knees and elbows.

Pat learns about an online expert system that can be used at home to find out more about these problems.

(*a*) The expert system could be evaluated by its purpose and *domain* of expertise.

(i) State the "domain" of this expert system. **1**

(ii) State **one other** characteristic that could be used to evaluate the expert system. **1**

(*b*) Two methods of inferencing that can be used in an expert system are *forward chaining* and *backward chaining*.

(i) Explain what is meant by "forward chaining" and "backward chaining". **2**

(ii) Describe **one** advantage of using forward chaining in this expert system. **2**

(6)

Total for Section III Part B (25)

[*END OF SECTION III—PART B—EXPERT SYSTEMS*]

Marks

SECTION III

PART C—The Internet

Attempt ALL questions in this section.

18. Ray is configuring the latest version of an e-mail client to send and receive his e-mail. The e-mail client uses POP and SMTP protocols.

(*a*) State the purpose of POP and SMTP protocols. 2

(*b*) When this message is transmitted over the Internet, it is divided into *packets*.

Explain why the message is divided into packets. 2

(*c*) The e-mail client inserts Ray's contact details at the end of each e-mail.

> Ray Tomlison
> 111 Mains Water Road
> Glasgow
> E-mail: R.Tomlison@parpanet.org
> Tel: 0141 496 0001
> Fax: 0141 496 0002

(i) State **one** reason why Ray includes contact details in the e-mail. 1

(ii) Describe **one** concern Ray might have about including his contact details at the end of the e-mail. 1

(*d*) Ray is concerned that a virus could be downloaded as an e-mail attachment.

Suggest **two** methods of reducing the risk of a virus infecting Ray's computer. 2

(8)

19. Chumms.com is a social networking website that allows friends to keep in touch when online.

(*a*) Name the Internet service that allows friends to communicate in real-time. 1

(*b*) Chumms.com allows members to share photographs. Photographs are uploaded to the member's profile page.

Name the protocol used to upload a photo. 1

(*c*) Many schools have blocked the Chumms website to prevent pupils from accessing it.

(i) Suggest **one** reason why schools have blocked this website. 1

(ii) Suggest **one** reason why pupils should be allowed access to Chumms.com. 1

(4)

[Turn over

Marks

20. The diagram below shows a school Web page.

(*a*) The layout of the Web page above has been defined using the table tool. The menu allows you to navigate from this page to other pages and the graphic animates when the pointer is moved over it.

(i) State the feature of the Web authoring software which has been used to create the menu. **1**

(ii) A *scripting tool* has been used to animate the graphic.

Describe what is meant by a "scripting tool". **1**

(*b*) Here is the website file structure for www.school.sch.uk.

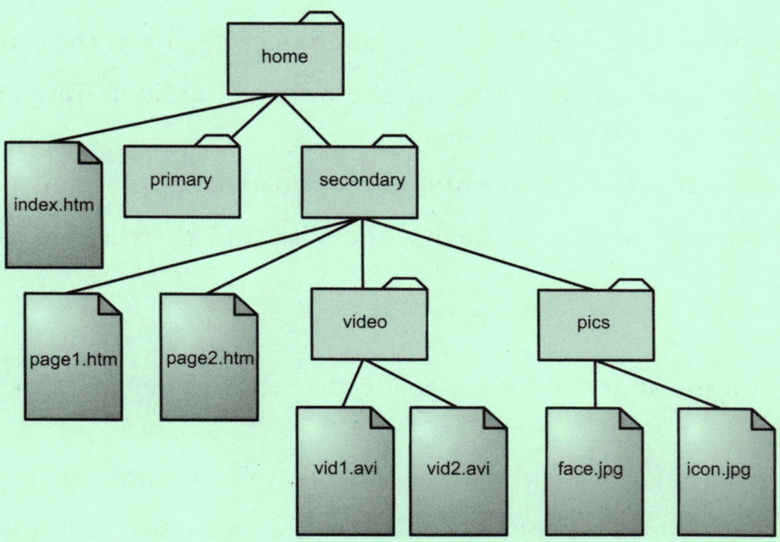

John is adding links to the **page1.htm** Web page.

(i) State the absolute address John will enter on page1.htm to link to face.jpg. **2**

(ii) State the relative address John will enter on page1.htm to link to icon.jpg. **1**

(*c*) Explain why picture compression is used on a website. **2**

(*d*) A browser is used to navigate from one page to another.

Name the facility of a browser which allows you to store a Web address for later access. **1**

(8)

Marks

21. Emma's favourite band is MacFlee. She is using a search engine to find the title of MacFlee's first song.

(*a*) State a Boolean search that could be entered by Emma to find this information. **3**

(*b*) Emma wishes to listen to MacFlee's first song. Describe how Emma could use the advanced features of a search engine to find the song file. **1**

(*c*) When Emma selects one of the websites suggested by the search engine, several pop-up windows appear. Name the type of software you would recommend Emma installs to prevent the pop-up windows. **1**

(5)

Total for Section III Part C (25)

[*END OF SECTION III—PART C—THE INTERNET*]

[*END OF QUESTION PAPER*]

[BLANK PAGE]

[BLANK PAGE]

[BLANK PAGE]